T0149179

The Woman THAT I AM

A POETRY DIARY

VANNESSA P. JAMES

authorHOUSE®

AuthorHouse™
1663 Liberty Drive
Bloomington, IN 47403
www.authorhouse.com
Phone: 1 (800) 839-8640

Published by AuthorHouse   10/04/2016

ISBN: 978-1-5246-4303-4 (sc)
ISBN: 978-1-5246-4301-0 (hc)
ISBN: 978-1-5246-4302-7 (e)

Library of Congress Control Number: 2016916491

Print information available on the last page.

This book is printed on acid-free paper.

*This is dedicated to my biggest fan,
my dad, my friend.*

VICTOR JAMES

Contents

Preface

What you are about to read is a collection of thoughts, emotions, and experiences that span a little more than twenty years of my life. Some are my personal experiences. Others are whispered words and special request to pen something that they themselves felt yet couldn't express as eloquently as they would have liked. (Please know that each one has read his or her special piece and approved it.) And in doing so, they shared a piece of themselves with me and helped to shape my destiny.

It's taken me a long time to decide to put these into print. I hope that you find joy, tears, solace, release, and love in these lines. I encourage you to write you own thoughts in the journal pages provided. Your words may someday help someone else through their own situation or to understand you. It may even help you understand you. These writings continue to help me now.

I know I'm speaking as though I didn't write these poems myself. I did write them but always with the knowledge that God was guiding me. I am but the instrument and I am pleased to be so.

I would also like to take this opportunity to thank those who helped organize and edit this collection. To Ms. Karina Tatesovyan, Mr. and Mrs. Patrick Sa, and all the others who supported my effort to share this gift, I love you the more. True friendship has been weighed, measured, tested, and proven by your honesty.

With that said, I wish you safe journey. I know you will reach the other side in victory.

Who Am I?

Sometimes I sit and gaze at this face
This face in which I see so much
The cheekbones that sit high and proud; strength on display
Lips full of the promise of wisdom passed from generation to generation
A nose, not too thin nor too wide, bringing a necessary balance
And eyes that are windows to the soul, aged and ageless
This is a face to love, that I love
A reflection of the inner person
Sometimes I sit and gaze at this face
And I smile at my own reflection

Nature

I am as wild as nature could ever be.
Untamed by no one, but myself.
A spirit of wild heart and willful soul.

At home, am I, amongst the beauty of nature for wildlife is as uncontainable as I.
To own us is a chore, and in the end, never accomplished.

Like the volcano, I erupt with substances to add to my amorously impenetrable foundation.
Substances that will, in time, be as strong as my unconscious soul.

Like the earthquakes am I, able to shake one to the awareness of the reality of fantasy.
The world is made of dreams.

Like tornado am I, twisting with a gentle fury made of love.
Special are those protected within my center.

Like the hurricane am I, ironically blowing with colorful moods which are mine.
A ferocious calm, then a silent storm.

I am Nature unstained.
Therefore, I am an "Unconditional Spirit".
A spirit of wild heart and willful soul.

Essence

Beneath the darkness of angry despair, a soul withers under the weight. How much longer can it endure? A soul once strong with eccentric vitality, drained. Sapped of willfulness, a gradual loss of uniqueness. That nature which was vivacious has become almost absolute with that of oblivion. Depression.

What gave Soul its vitality? Ah, yes. It is the flowers whether they bloom or not. The sky, in all its magnificent colors, exposing each mood. The mountains, which stand tall, immovable, illuminated with their own pride. The animals guided by instinct, stand tall, cunning, and their wild unyielding attempts to do the impossible…survive MANkind. And still there is more… the sea with all its fury and calm, unconcerned with humanity, but mothering waves its grass in the wind testing the intellectual integrity of MANkind. Then there is Time.

Time. It has no beginning or end; and yet, both in abundance. Time is nothing and/or something. It is structure, but made of no tangible substance. Time is a contradiction by which we measure vitality. Like the Soul, it rules and is ruled by that undermined need which lingers in the balance. An unconscious, unsuspected need buried within the normalcy of every day living. The need for which there is no cure. Or is there?

What is this need? How can one know it when one sees it? Where can it be found? Is it a feasible "thing of MANkind"? Or simply out of mortal reach? Will it be familiar, vague or just unknown? So many questions, but so few, if any, answers.

A quest begins. For those who embark upon such a journey, it is one riddle, one face, with a multitude of variations, and yet, one answer. Perhaps it will present itself, the Essence of the Soul. The key that brings vitality and strength back to the Soul. Perhaps Self-love is the Essence of the Soul. What will you find at your journey's end? Will it be the needed Essence?

In the Silence of Death

Trust? I can't live without it
Not being trusted by a friend
Makes them no longer my friend

It is difficult for me to be around
For fear of being left out
Although I am very different
We are very much alike

This has shown me quite a lot
And for my age, I am young
But, for my mind, I am old
In the same time, you have
Shown me almost all of yourself
Yet now, who are you?
For an instance, I know you
In another, I know you not

You seem to find refuge in those
Who would ultimately betray you
Yet manage to think wrongly of me
Because of something you think I've done

How you feel no longer matters
I have changed for the better
Or perhaps the worse
How I feel no longer matters
We speak not to one another
Our secrets are all forgotten
I wish you health and happiness
Amongst your "others"
As I find myself
In the silence of death

Peace! Be Still

My mind?! The violence, the pain. What's going on inside of my head? I want to express my feelings, but what are they? I am lost in a storm of thoughts. I can't find my way out. NO! I must think positive. There must be a way to clear my mind of all this. The beach! The ocean! The wind!... but how can I get there? Through the mind, use my mind against itself. My memory.

PEACE! Be Still

I remember the roar of the ocean, the crash of the waves speaking in a rhythmic voice talking to me soothing the savage storm of thoughts. I can feel the wind caressing my soul. Strange, yet...so familiar. There is something about the creations of God, something that simply rules out the creations of MANkind.

PEACE! Be Still

The beach, it makes me think. The ocean, it talks to me. The wind, it holds me. The mountains, they listen to me. The birds, they sing to me. The prairies, they give me rest. The animals, they teach me strength. The rain, it cries with me. The lightening, it reaches inside of me. The clouds, they make me smile. The stars, they show me how to dream. The moonlight, it reminds me that I am unique. The dark, it teaches me not to be afraid. And the snow, for it teaches me how to love in the midst of the coldness of huMANity....

PEACE! Be Still

One

There comes a time in life when One's only refuge is to crawl into a corner, curl up, and mummify. One's time has come.

Here One lies in a cobwebbed corner with an emotional tidal wave building inside. A struggle between controlled and uncontrolled. A battle One wins, and loses. To be victorious as well as defeated; how does One feel? Is One happy and sad? Angry, envious, conceited, self-righteous, hurt, sympathetic?.... Confusion is the end result.

But how can One find peace after such a war? Even confusion causes tension; therefore, tension will rise, and once again, war. Is this kind of war endless? Does One have any hope of "calm"? One has heard that it is calmest before the storm, but is the "calm" that which One desires or deception? Even though it appears to be peaceful, is it? No. One has witnessed such occurrences. One knows these aches, pains......

Wounded within. Knocked down. Knocked down. Willingly caught unaware by illusion. All caused by an unnatural instinct bred into One by One's own ancestry. Century after century. Yet, One will not be given in to despair.

An age old battle has begun and ended to begin again. And still, One will overcome to let it be "calm".

In remembrance of my grandfather, Marvin Johnson

Mere Existence

Today is a day of days upon days
It would seem with no beginning and no end in sight
A vague memory of birth
A feeling of now... A heavy burden

Tomorrow will be a row of urgencies
An even growing tide of things
Things that need to be done
A tide never to reach the shores of completion
A tiring exercise... A weary thought

Yesterday serves as a reminder
Allowing yourself to look back down Life's Mountain to Earth
Instead of up to the Life's Peak
Seeing only the clouds below gently sailing past
A thankful determination...A need to just be

Love

Daddy's Promises

When I came into this world
>   You held me in your arms and promised to protect me

When I began to understand
>   You promised to teach me all that you knew

When I began to imagine
>   You promised to show me how to make my dreams reality

When I began to venture into the world
>   You promised to be there should I ever need to come home

When I was ready for freedom
>   You promised to let go of me yet never release me from your love

And now I can look back and know that you've kept every promise
>   Now I promise to never let go of all that you given to me

Written on Father's Day, Sunday, June 17, 2007

I Love the Way You Love Me

I love the way you smile when I catch you watching me
With a little sheepish chuckle and a sparkle in your eyes

I love the way you reach for me just to make sure I am near
With a protective concern that touches me deep within

I love the way you kiss my fingers, my neck, my cheek and then my lips
With a firm tenderness and a restrained passion that I feel with each kiss

I love the way you sigh when you hold me in your arms
With all of your body and soul, it pulls me closer than ever your arms can

I love the way you engage me in conversations for hours on end
With all the curiosity of a child and a worldly intelligence

I simply love the way you love me.

Sanctuary

I love how my skin looks against your skin
The blend of your darker hue against my slightly lighter one
The way they mingle, blend, and seem forever intertwined
As though our souls could play chase, going round and round
Like our loving that slows, then speeds, then slows again
A fulfilling circle,
No beginning
No end

Even the way that I cradle into you
You holding me firmly to you
I can feel your heart beat against mine
I can hear the new rhythm of mine and yours, entrancing me
Enthralling me, taking me on a journey through the depths of you
An erotic trip,
Your mind
Your soul

What can I say to keep you talking to me?
Your velvet lips send words to play around my ears
The small deep laugh that vibrates through my body
The way your eyes dance as intellect turns you on
The seriousness of your conversation that becomes passion
Exposing your soul
My soul
Our passion

As we twist and turn through the winding roads
Our conversation takes on a new language
Words have run out to be replaced by something stronger
A fire has been ignited causing our bodies to relate without words
Your darker hue against my slightly lighter one
Just the beginning
Just sparks
Now flames

Through the flames, we race even faster, ever further
To a place of heightened senses, of only feelings
Now I know what it feels like to be aware of every touch
Of every breath, every sound, and even the slightest movement
There is nothing in this place except you and I
In this place
We created
Our sanctuary

Here or There?

It's a shame that when I was here
You were there
Now that you are here
It's time for me to go there
But now that we have spent time here
I am torn between here
And there
Why couldn't you have been here?
Or I, there?
While I stand here
The future is waiting for me there
And I am torn between here
And there
Wondering if I should go to "my" there
And longing to stay here
I can't help but ponder the idea of you, here
Of me following you from here
To "your" there
But will Fate allow "my" here
To become "your" there?
Can I alter the path to "my" there?
Why can't we both go to another there?
Create our own there?
A fine line between here
And there…

We would never survive that kind of there

But can we survive this kind of here?

The truth is that when I am here
You will always be there
And when I am there
You will always be here
But times will occur when here and there...

And now...

Good-bye

I can't take back what I feel
I can't help wanting you
I can't fight to have it all

I'll just kiss you

I can't explore the possibilities of us
I can't turn my back on what's right
I can't be anyone but me

I'll just kiss you

I can't accept your limitations
I can't be bound without commitment
I can't stand the contradicting confusion

I'll just kiss you…

Good-bye

Passing of Time

You had me and didn't know it
You had me and I couldn't show it
You had me wrapped around your finger
You could have told me anything
It would have been anything for you

I was afraid of what would happen
I was afraid to let myself completely fall
I was afraid to hurt again
I couldn't take another devastating love pain
It would have been too much for me

With wary eyes, I could see the differences
With wary eyes, I could see the future problems
With wary eyes, I refused to listen to the reasons why I should
I could have listened half-heartedly
It would have happened for us then

You had me but you didn't feel my intensity
I was afraid to seek sanctuary
With wary eyes, we could have seen the comfort of us
We could have loved and been loved
It would have been a tender passing of time

Yearning

They say that women have that biological clock thing
Ticking and waiting for that day a child is formed in their bodies
But not I…that would be a result of my true desire
A desire for true unconditional love

For that someone who will love me as I am
Daddy's little girl, giggling teenager,
Sexy rebellious twenty-something, or vivacious lady
No matter which, still all woman

For that someone who is that man that I can love
Protective big brother, independent youngster
Handsome sweet talker or strong sensitive lover
No matter which, still my man

Sharing our secrets, planning our future
Strengthening each other's souls with sweet words of encouragement
Hand in hand dancing to life's music
In step as though we had one heartbeat moving in the fluidness of our love

Knowing each others thoughts and yet still learning all about us
Our weaknesses made strong in our unity
The core of our lives is God and our family a gift of joy; a blessing
Our struggles made worth while; sweeter

I'm yearning for something different
Something not easily found nor won
I'm yearning for that someone special
Someone who's yearning for someone like me.

Fate's Vision

I often look at you and wonder what it is that makes me feel this way...

Then I see your smile, the depth in your eyes, and the "what could be"

I even try to ignore the way I feel only to have others who know me best say what my heart already knows...

I can't help but to think of you at the most inappropriate of moments

Whether shopping or walking, simply watching TV or mid-sentence, there is you...

What ever shall I do?

Something to have and not to have...

So close and still so far

The love that is and can't be...

Shall I look down the "Road of Possibilities"?

How can I when I have convinced myself that it will never be with all the reasoning of my mind...

Even in spite of my stubbornly closed eyes, my heart refuses to be blinded

With a Heart's glance, I see with Fate's vision that our paths will end on the same road...

Now, with a soul felt sigh, I look at you and wonder what it is that makes me feel this way...

Then I see your smile, the depth in your eyes, and the "what could be"

Suddenly

Suddenly thoughts of you randomly pop into my head
I wonder if you would like this outfit with these shoes
If you would like this fedora in deep blue or maybe green to wear
Oooo tickets to the Raiders' game, would you go?

Suddenly my mind is full of vacation thoughts for two
I was thinking of going off to Maui alone but now
It's "I have to make sure the hotel is on the beach
So he can hear the waves while I watch him drift off to sleep."

Suddenly, I am shaking my head with a smile and a chuckle
Is he thinking the same way or am I really just doing "too much"
Is he thinking a year out? 5 years from now? 10?
Is he thinking, "if this works out, we are going to be so happy!"

Suddenly, my mind and heart are agreeing on the possibilities
Seeing the shadows of good things to come
Willing to take the good with the bad and still make it work
Seeing what it feels like to want to fall in love
                    ...suddenly

Touched

I have to say that your words have touched the chords in my heart
Strings that have only been looked at
Admired from a distance
Kept silent by choice and always just out of reach
Where the only sound that can be heard
Are faint whispers hidden in the distant memories of the past
Of love wins and love losses
Of love wishes and will bes
Of love don'ts and love won'ts
Of love completely and so sweetly
These are the sounds of me
Of what has made me strong
Of family dedication
Of Blessings from on High
Of my unfound soul mate
Your words sent out a perfect note
A smooth melody is starting to form
Off to a slow steady rhythm
Listen closely Maestro…
It's my heartbeat

Whisper of Love

Once I heard a Whisper of Love
The joy it brought was so unexpected
It came at a time when I thought I would never want it

Love whispered and I hushed

As my heart and mind became still
I listened to the sweet words that came
They carried warmth and the soft caress of confidence

Love whispered and I sighed

The whisper called to my soul
My soul, it called back and came running
Even as my soul ran, it whispered back

Love whispered and my soul whispered too

Then silence came from somewhere
Nowhere in particular, just there
My heart and mind sank back into the rhythm

Love did not whisper and my soul longed

Sometimes I catch traces on the wind
Or catch a breath of it, so sweet and gentle
And as I turn to whisper, it fades in to the air

When Love whispers, I will whisper back

Choice

Here is a place of logical and illogical

A place where fantasy becomes reality, then fantasy again

Here is what draws them to the unknown understanding

The beginning of an obsession of pride, of desire to win

Here is a place where the unseen controls and is uncontrolled

The seen striving to be free; yet, longing to remain passive

Here is what sets them apart from others, the Test

Of what they are tested the Place knows naught and is left naïve

Here is a place that perhaps is not a place

Yet a sacred Place just the same

Here is what; what is here

We even know it and may call it

By

Name

My Thoughts

Sometimes my thoughts wander from place to place

They look back to a beautiful day clear and sunny
A place where the earth and sea meet
The thunder of the waves still echo in my ears at the thought
Maybe I'll go back there

Other times my thoughts wander from person to person

They took me back to the first of my loves
The love meant to last that ended too soon
A life from that love never to be seen
But to prepare for the next love to come
I hope he knows how much I care

Sometimes my thoughts wander from feeling to feeling

They took me deep into my soul to a place I don't often go
A hidden door locked against the hardened side of my heart
With the heat of anger pulsing
I pray it never opens

How Much

How much to want somebody so it hurts with every passing thought –
Scream the pain

How much to keep someone happy at all cost to yourself –
Your life's blood

How much to know that somebody holds your heart and soul in the palm of
their hands
Your trust in them

How much to need someone to hold you in their arms the way only they can –
Run to them

How much to never give somebody all that they deserve –
The mercy within

How much…
How much…

Struggling to Understand

All my life I have struggled to understand
To comprehend your words which speak with double meaning
The "do as I say, not as I do" syndrome

I have wondered why you think your parenting doesn't start until you actually see me
But ends when I reach the age of 19
Unless you feel the need for control in the situation

I have yet to understand why you think your explanations are without question;
The coup de grâce; the end all, be all
But mine, as a child and even now, are ripped apart and pieced together: interrogated

My comprehension of things in the world is much clearer
I have taken the time to see for myself
I know that I must understand me before I can understand you

When will you understand you?
That you may have better vision, not 20-20, but thinking vision
Or will you always settle for the honey-glazed reasoning of least resistance

Will you always think only from your point of understanding?
Or will you consider as many angles as possible?
Or will you continue in this circle that follows itself round and round?

I hope for you
I pray for you
I am beginning to understand you
                              So I will not make the same faux pas

How I feel

Do you even listen to how I feel?
   Do you truly hear how I feel?
      Without bias, how I feel?

Not from someone else how I feel
   But from me how I feel
      With your own unadulterated feelings feel how I feel

It would seem you prefer how I feel
   From second and third parties how I feel
      A clouded over version of how I feel

The tainted tale of how I feel
   Mixed with their opinions of how I feel
      But then, even you choose how I feel

Never taken at face value for how I feel
   More speculation and suspicion of how I feel
      A conspiracy on all your parts how I feel

Causing me to put up a wall around how I feel
   Needing to seek refuge how I feel
      Pushed to tears how I feel

Screaming how I feel
           Being told to my face how I feel
                      Wrong of you how I feel

But you never really care how I feel
           It is not truly about how I feel
                      More about how you feel about how I feel

Too afraid of the truth of how I feel
           Can't face your own feelings to how I feel
                      You know in your heart how I feel

That caused now how I feel
           But now I can never tell you how I feel
                      Because of your illusions of how I feel

But not just for me about how I feel
           And I still am how I feel
                      No matter what, it's how I feel

Tomorrow I Find Peace

Today,

    My heart aches...

The wound I thought had started to heal has suddenly given forth a staggering pain
It would seem that it has opened again
As if it has managed to be a deeper wound than I expected
As if something or someone does not want it to heal

Today,

    My soul cries...

The sound came from everywhere and nowhere all of sudden
But as a whisper that grew to a scream expected but not truly wanted
It brings to silence that wailing from within
It seems as if it will not stop and does
It carries a promise to come again if ignored

Today,

    My mind soars...

With the thoughts of what to do to calm the scream and ease the pain
How to close the wound and remove the poison that seems to inhabit it
Where to find a cure that will stop the screaming and the flood in my soul
Thoughts of my heart, my soul... my heart...my soul, my head...

Tomorrow,
> I find peace...

It's there just beyond my fingertips held ever so tightly in my heart
Shimmering faintly at the edge of my soul wanting to clear a path through my thoughts
PEACE I seek and will find
Tomorrow I shall wear it like my own skin
Tomorrow it shall protect me from that day on...

Today,
> I have chaos

Tomorrow,
> I find peace

Return to Self

Truly, I understand
The Heart,
    The Pain,
        The Aches

            Erasing a hopeful gain
                And unsuccessful memories

Truly, I understand
The Tears,
    The Wonders,
        The Expression

            Losing the will to love
                Only to gain no life

Truly, I understand
The Feelings,
    The Fears,
        The Hurt

            But for you to understand
                Is for you to return to self

In my hour of desperation

I was lost, confused
I was struggling, hungry
I was tired, homeless

No idea how I got there

In my hour of desperation

I became hateful, angry
I became a liar, cheating
I became unknown, alone

No idea of who or what I was

In my hour of desperation

I called a friend, an acquaintance
I called an enemy, a cohort
I called my family, a distant relative

No idea of who I could rely on

In my hour of deliverance

I was crazy, delirious
I became frantic, hysterical
I called on Jesus, the Lord

And was unburdened of myself

Crossroad of Choice

The time has come for change
>Perhaps the most important choice of a lifetime

What will prevail of it, one may ask?
>Which is stronger of mind and passion?

Will it be the one name for it?
>Or the one who seeks it for personal gain?

The battle of the subconscious…
>A perfect name for a hidden war; or is it hidden?

Who shall win, one may ask again?
>Strength or wit: power or knowledge

Or will power alone be enough?
>Will knowledge take on a new aura in the heat of battle?

Choose or be chosen; conquer or be conquered
>Fail, and what shall come may not be to one's liking

But win, and all shall be as one will have it
>Yet, which will be the merciful of the two?

Yes, the time has come for change
>The most important choice to be made for one's self

Will one be chosen to choose to conquer?
>Or choose to be chosen and be conquered?

The choice is one's own,
>And it will own that one…Forever…

My Own Direction

Today I went my own way on my own

I found that I was happy alone on my own

That it was not I who needed a companion

But a companion who needed me

Tomorrow I shall go my own way again

For the direction I go will be my own

Spiritual

Beloved

I spent my past begging to be loved
To be wanted not just needed

To have a pitying kind of love is degrading
But it would seem all that I am capable of receiving

Or the jealous kind of love not fiercely protective of me,
But a hateful love given begrudgingly to hurt me, punish me

It is ever "Poor little girl, throw her some love scraps."
Or "Woman with love strength to spare, give all you can and more"

Drained, tired, weak, shamed, wiped,
Threatened, hated and hunted

Why must I be perfection?
Never had I claimed to be nor have I wanted to be

My slightest err is made into an overwhelming irreversible unforgivable wrong
Will it ever be so?

Even when the wrong was never mine to begin with
My wrong was always the desire to keep others from feeling the same

From feeling that pain born from the inconsiderate
Birthing me, the unlovable, the undesirable, the "un"

I have been all and nothing
To everyone and no one

I have no longer the need to beg for love
For my soul has ever been kind in its treatment of you and me

Glory be to God for the molding of such a soul
For the gift He gave that stands firm against you and even me

Now I take the peace that is rightfully mine
Now I am beloved of myself

Beloved of the ultimate Love
Beloved of God

Jeanine's Prayer

Just as the Lord loves me, so shall I love myself
Even in the face of Adversity for it will be vanquished
As each day dawns, I will keep my eyes to the Heavens
Nothing can withstand the Will of God, and
I stand anchored forever in my Savior, the Lover of my soul
Needing only His Love, His Acceptance, His Guidance, and His Mercy
Everlasting. Amen

Encouragement From Within

Today is the last day of a past life.
Of a dying, now dead, part of me.
Of the worst part of my life.

Tomorrow, a new beginning. A whole new me.
The alternative to lifelessness is the awakening to reality.
The new breath of life given once more.

A resurrection of mind, body, and soul.
Of a heart which was thought to never love again.
And of an intelligence superior to that of old.

My promise, my way, my goal
To be achieved by my desire.
The truth within me is a pure white dove soaring freely.

Ty's Prayer

Sometimes, late at night, when the pain and confusion is too much to bare
I cry...
And I cry out
Why me, Lord?

I shed tears from the pain of the weight on my soul until I can cry no more
Then I ...
Begin to pray

Please Lord bring the light of day
I no longer want to feel this way
Please Lord send the Holy Spirit
I just don't know if I can make it through

And afterwards, I look down the road, through the valley, and the way is still long and dark
But I know...
I will make it
To the other side

So now I pray in the blessings of day and in the sorrows of night
But this...
Is how I pray

I thank you Lord for one more day
I thank you Lord even for feeling this way
I thank you Lord for the Holy Spirit
For now I look back and know I made it through

All the Time

I went to the top of a mountain
And called His Name
But got no answer

I went to the ocean
And looked as far as the eye could see
But did not see Him

I went to the valley
And searched its depths
But did not find Him

I went to the church
And ran from room to room
And wondered "Why isn't He here?"

I searched from city to city
Dawn to dawn
And still could not find Him

I asked everyone I saw
    They shared what they knew
        But their answers were not enough

In desperation, I sat down, withdrew into myself
    And moaned with all the pain in my soul
        "Lord, where are you?"

And He answered
    And He said
        "I have been with you all the time"

Then the pain eased
    My tears fell
        And peace came

Now I know He will be with me all the time

The Cleansing Fire

When you have run as far and as fast as you can
When your soul has became a barren desert
When your mind can no longer distinguish this from that

　　The Fire Cometh

When you've reached a point when you can no longer sleep
When you hear voices in your head in constant argument
When you can no longer shed a tear for self or anyone else

　　The Fire Cometh

When the Holy Spirit descends upon you like a cloud
When you are wrapped round with the thickness of it
When you feel there and not there all at once

　　The Fire has come

When the fire licks at the wounds hidden deep within you
When the scabs of pain and sores of misery start to disappear
When the veils of doubt, fear, and worry are torn down

The Fire has come

Because the Lord God has loved you
Because the Lord God has forgiven you
Because the Lord God has given His Son

The Cleansing Fire

Because the Lord God calls you back to Him
Because the Lord God opens the Heavens to bless you
Because the Lord God is the Great I Am

You have been through
        The Cleansing Fire

Redeemed

Now that the Lord has given me a new life, a new way of thinking
I must carry it all the day and the night
Through every aspect of my life from simply breathing to every action
24 hours a day, 365 days of each year as long as I live
Redeemed

But how will I stand against the wiles of my past? Stay Clean?
With the knowledge that God forgives and removes it from you
Know that the Blood of Christ that flows red washes you white
The Ultimate Life was given as full payment of your debt
Redeemed

Now that the Lord has given me sound ground to stand on
I must build on it a strong, sturdy, and lasting structure
Starting with the molding of my soul with the Word of God
To my very home that is my earthly shelter, lest it continually crumble and fall
Redeemed

But what will I do when I get tired and things get difficult
Remember that your strength comes from the Lord, He who never sleeps
"Trust in the Lord with all your heart, and lean not to your own understanding.
In all thy ways acknowledge Him, and He will direct your paths."[1]
Redeemed

Now that the Lord has made my body His Temple
I must treat it as I would treat the House of God
With vigilance and respect, simply put…. Watch and Pray
For the enemy comes but cannot stand against the Will of God
Redeemed

But how can I live as an example to a fallen world?
As Jesus is the Way and the Light unto you, so shall you be a beacon of light
in the world
Your destiny has been set as the stars in the skies to not only be….
Redeemed

But to redeem

[1] Proverbs 3:5, KJV

Humbly Invincible

Another age has dawned and with it I have received New Eyes
The will I once thought was my own I now know is truly the Will of God
I have always known that without Him I am nothing
And with Him, I am humbly invincible
Even through tears and the pain of the past, mine as well as others,
The long anxiety filled nights of waiting for daylight,
The times when things seemed to be coming from all,
The tense burden downed days that never seemed to end,
The times when I had to remind others that I had
not given up but choose to suffer in silence,
The realization of the foundation of faith that is in
me, and was in me, before I became me
The smiles that God brought me in the midst of the storm,
The anointing He has poured into and over my soul,
And the many ways He has used me to bless others and others to bless
me; I have always known that God had my path lain out before me
So with these New Eyes, I see the slow change the Lord has wrought in me
His Change, in His Time, always His Way, for His Purpose
I have always known that without Him I am nothing
And with Him, I am humbly invincible

The Woman That I Am

I would not be the woman that I am without the centuries of mothers that made me
Who raised me with their independent thinking, minds of their own
Who stood at my back and spoke the old wise tales, wisdom from their years of experience
Who taught me to respect the earth for God made it, showing me lost remedies of nature
Who told me that I must pass on the knowledge, one day you will be "MOTHER" too

I would not be the woman that I am without the life experiences of my years
All the times I chose not to listen and suffered because of it, a learning choice
All the times I heard and excelled, knowledge put into practice
All the times I tried every avenue I could and still wouldn't ask for help, a fierce independence
All the times I was able to proudly stand alone, a manifestation of the pride of my mothers

I would not be the woman that I am without the sisters who stand beside me
Who are should to shoulder with me, combining the strength of wills
Who encourage me when I have doubts about a chosen course, deepening the well of confidence
Who allow me to cry with openness unparalleled, reassuring with the hugs our mothers gave
Who help me in my time of need, showing the unity of the village that is our roots

I would not be the woman that I am without God in my life
> *He who knew me before I was, knows who I am, and guides me to the woman I will become*
> *He who gave me all that I needed to live this life everyday in His way*
> *He who birthed me into existence for a purpose that lies deep in my soul*
> *He who is in me, of me, around me, creating me, showing me that I am a Woman of His Making*

Else I would not be…
> *The woman that I am*

Printed in the United States
By Bookmasters